brexit

harris

brexit

corrupt press

other books by the same author

photography
plein (corrupt press, 2010)
la défense (corrupt press, 2012)
we print the truth (corrupt press, 2017)
none of the above (corrupt press, 2017)

poetry
europe (wurm press, 2008)
antwerp (wurm press, 2009)
the smoke (The Knives Forks and Spoons Press, 2011)
the liberation of [placeholder] (The Knives Forks and Spoons Press, 2012)
anticipating the metaverse (The Knives Forks and Spoons Press, 2014)
big town blues (The Knives Forks and Spoons Press, 2018)

Last century, I took some 35mm slides on various stock using a Pentax Me Super. They were stored for years in facilities that turned out to be damp. The now mouldy slides were scanned using a PlusTek Optic Film 8200i with Silverfast 8.8.0r7 running on an iMac 10,1 under El Capitan & Sierra. A bug in the scanning process added faux crystallisation. I prepared the results in Aperture 3.6.

the cover image is by the author
https://www.dylanharris.org/

979-10-90394-91-9
published by corrupt press
www.corruptpress.com

it's as though two trains ran through
in discordant sound / one a screeching
blackboard one a screeching bird /
these hard imagined fears were sharply pared
arthritis / the weather lightning stabbing
as though through bone on bone

a crowd of sixty million who talk in syn
chronie / tell acrimony things i couldn't
let me hear / four dead pets three cats a dog
said loud and strong the same / but i've
not heard nor understood that foul and
barking thing

for i won't hear divorce and hate for deeds
i haven't done / for i won't hear condemn
detest on things that don't exist / for i won't
hear my love has dreamt a hell and blamed
me for those dreams / for i've not met my love
for twenty years of peace

when mediamen make on line a psychopath
a mare / a cowering egg with arms on head
to shiver from the world / i did not think
it could be real but now that is my love

now that is my love

this poem was published in The Journal (www.thesamsmith.webs.com)

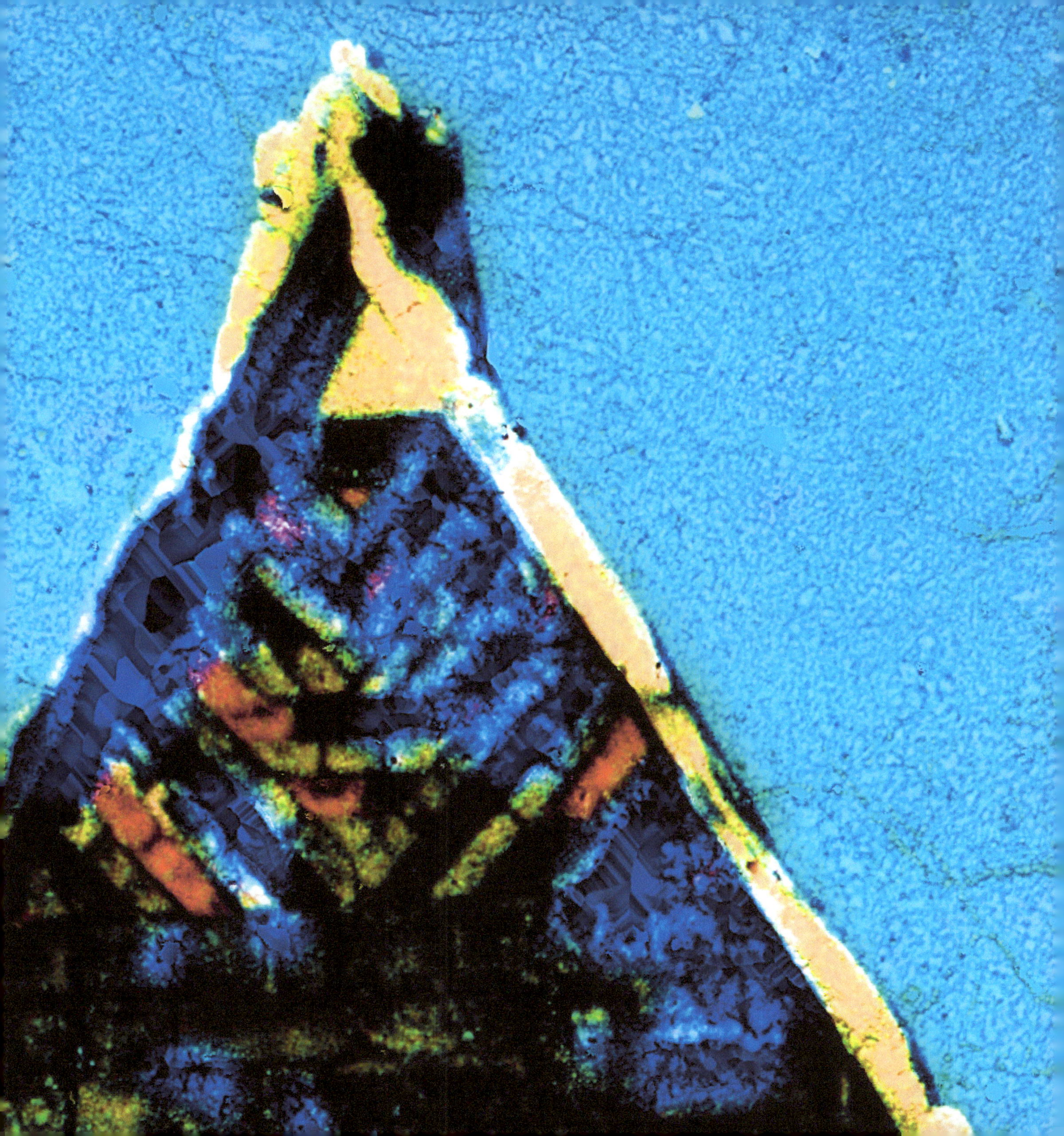

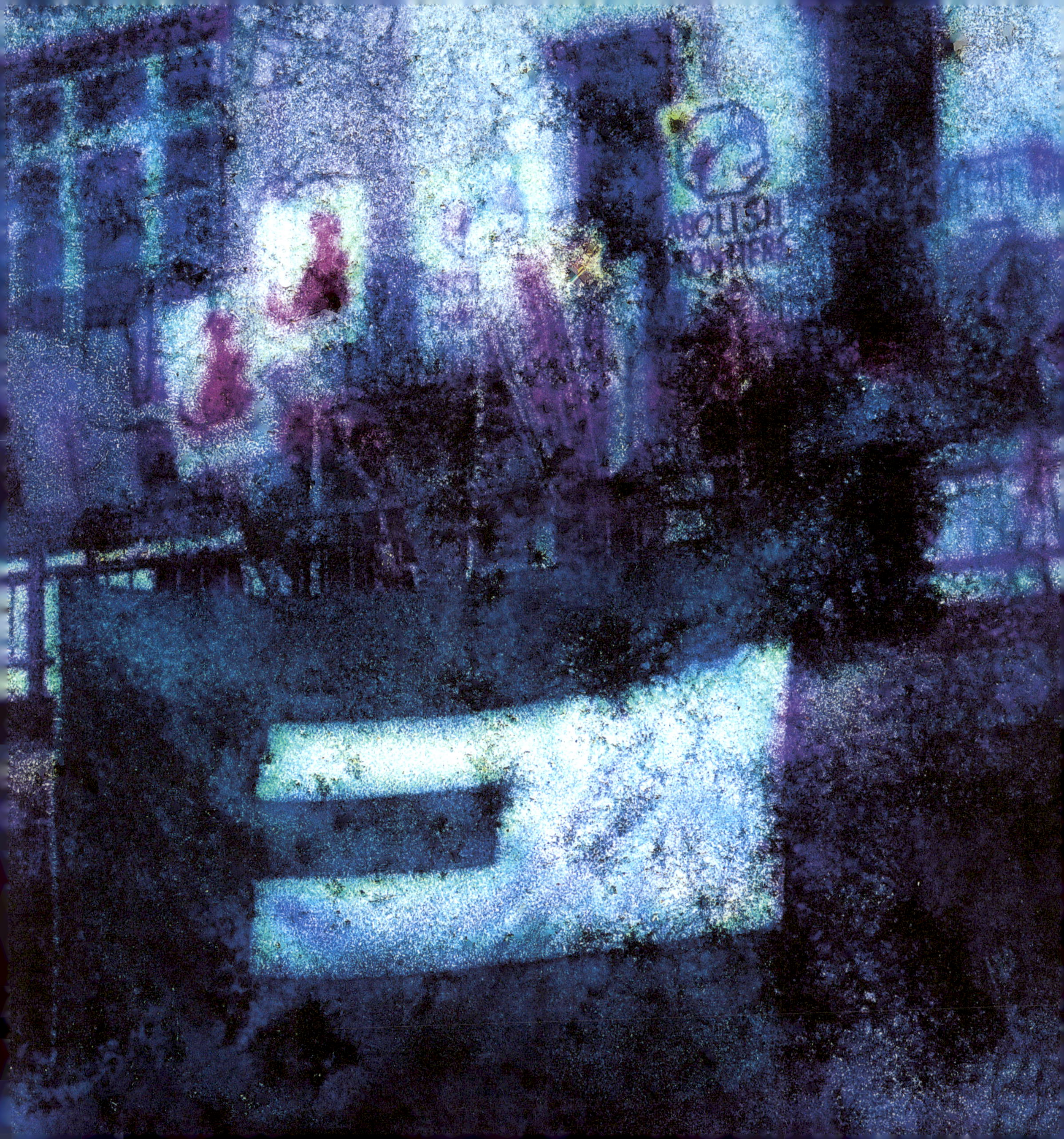

ABOLISH
BORDERS

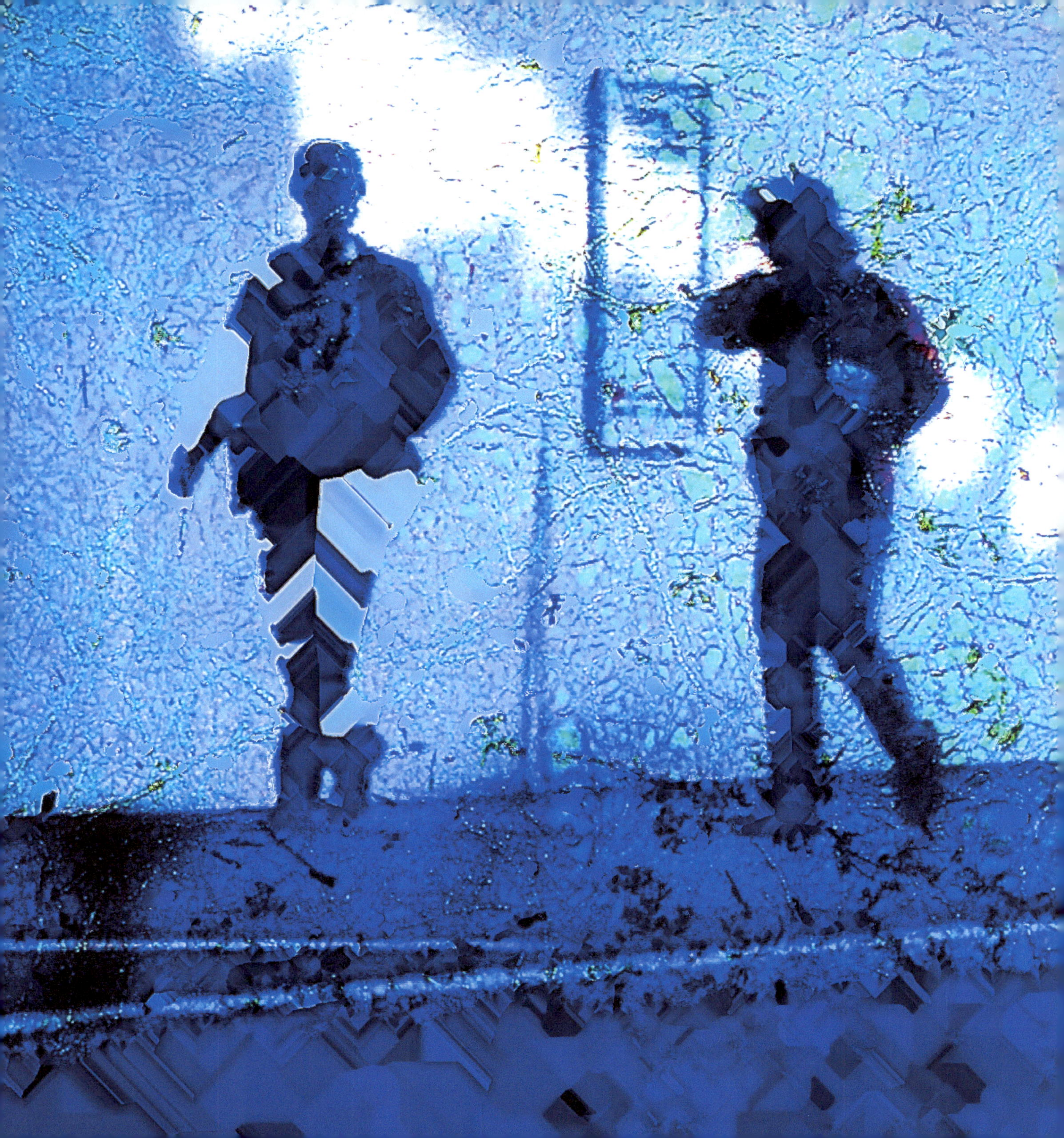

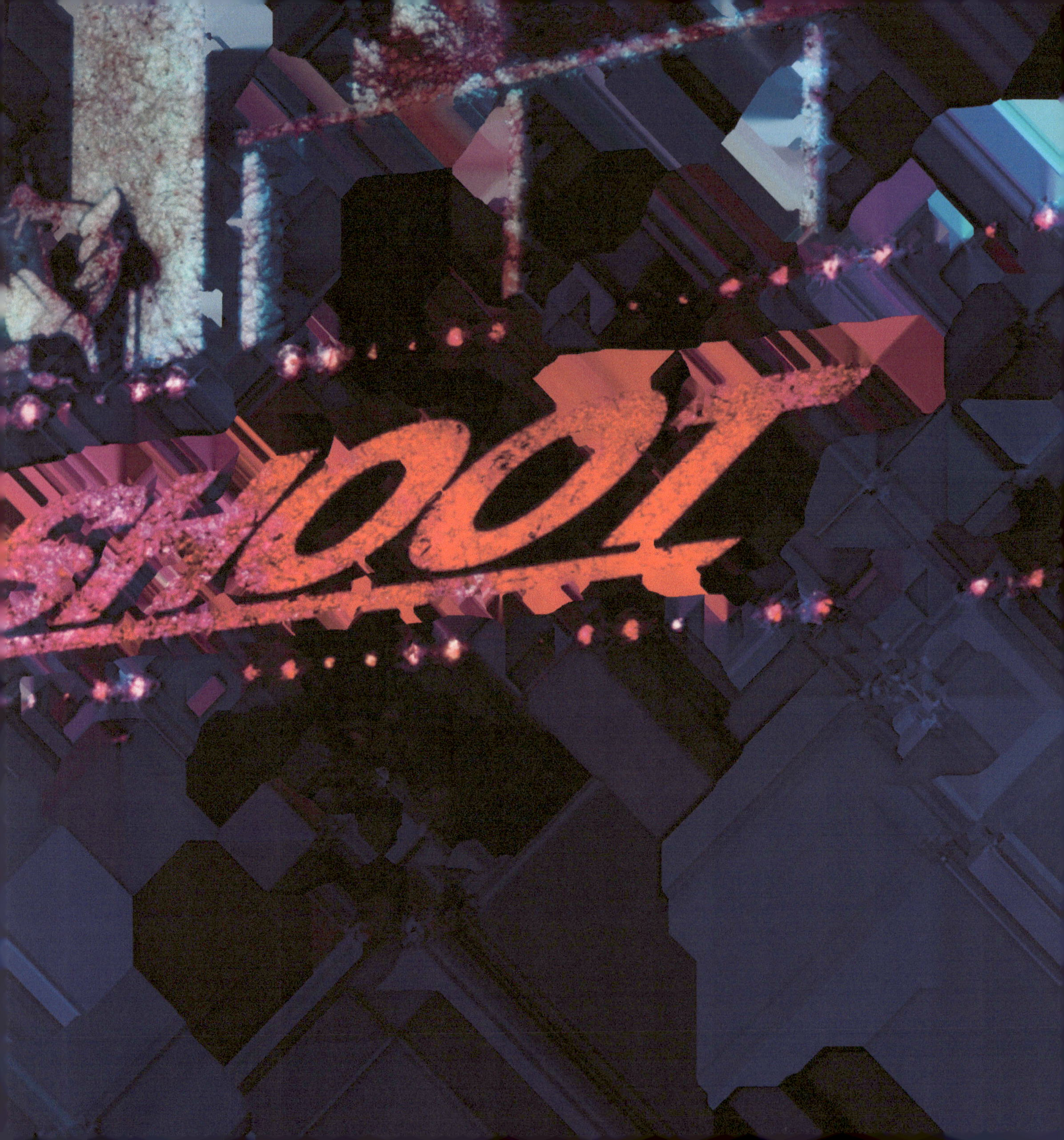

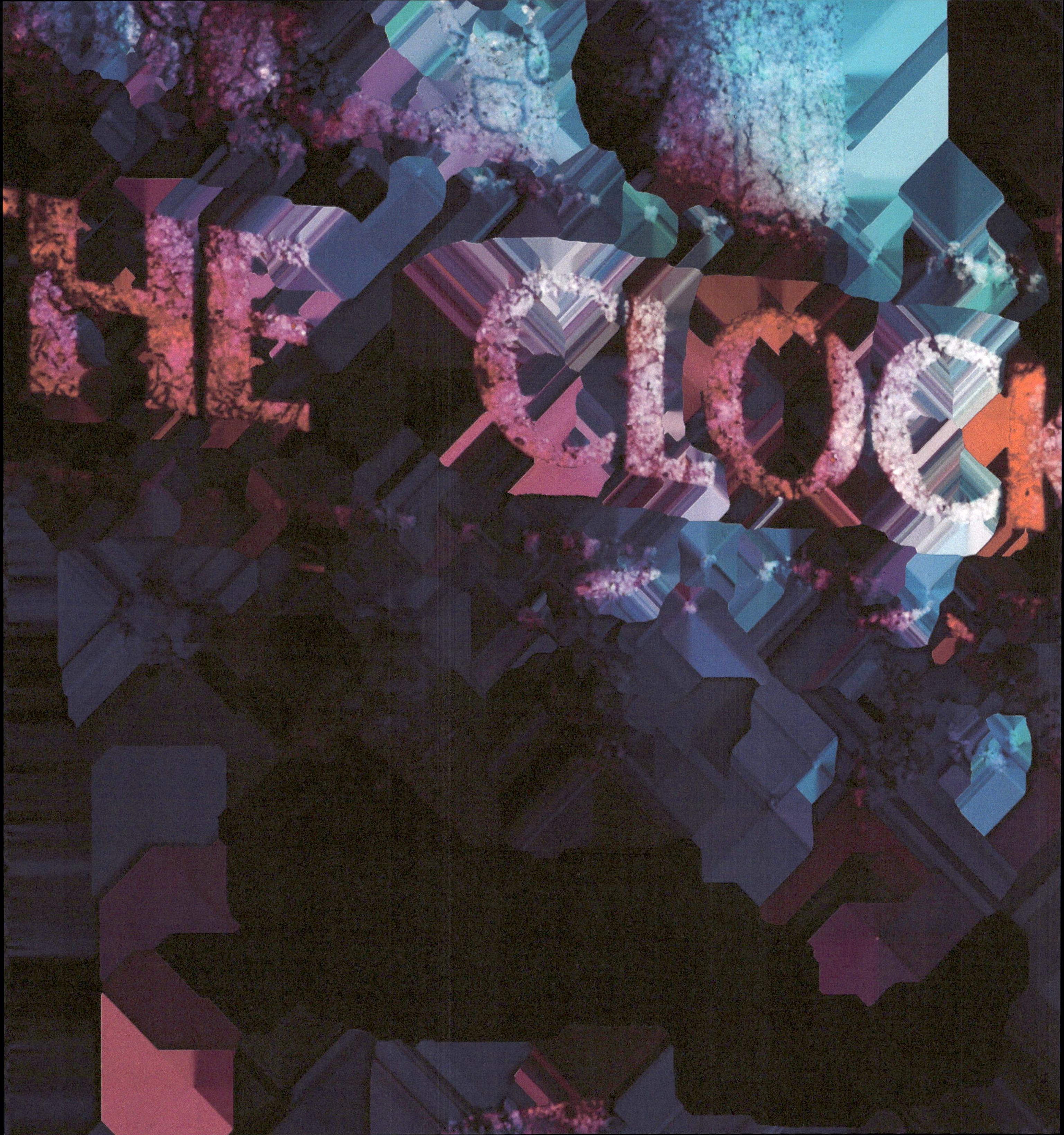

THE CLOCK

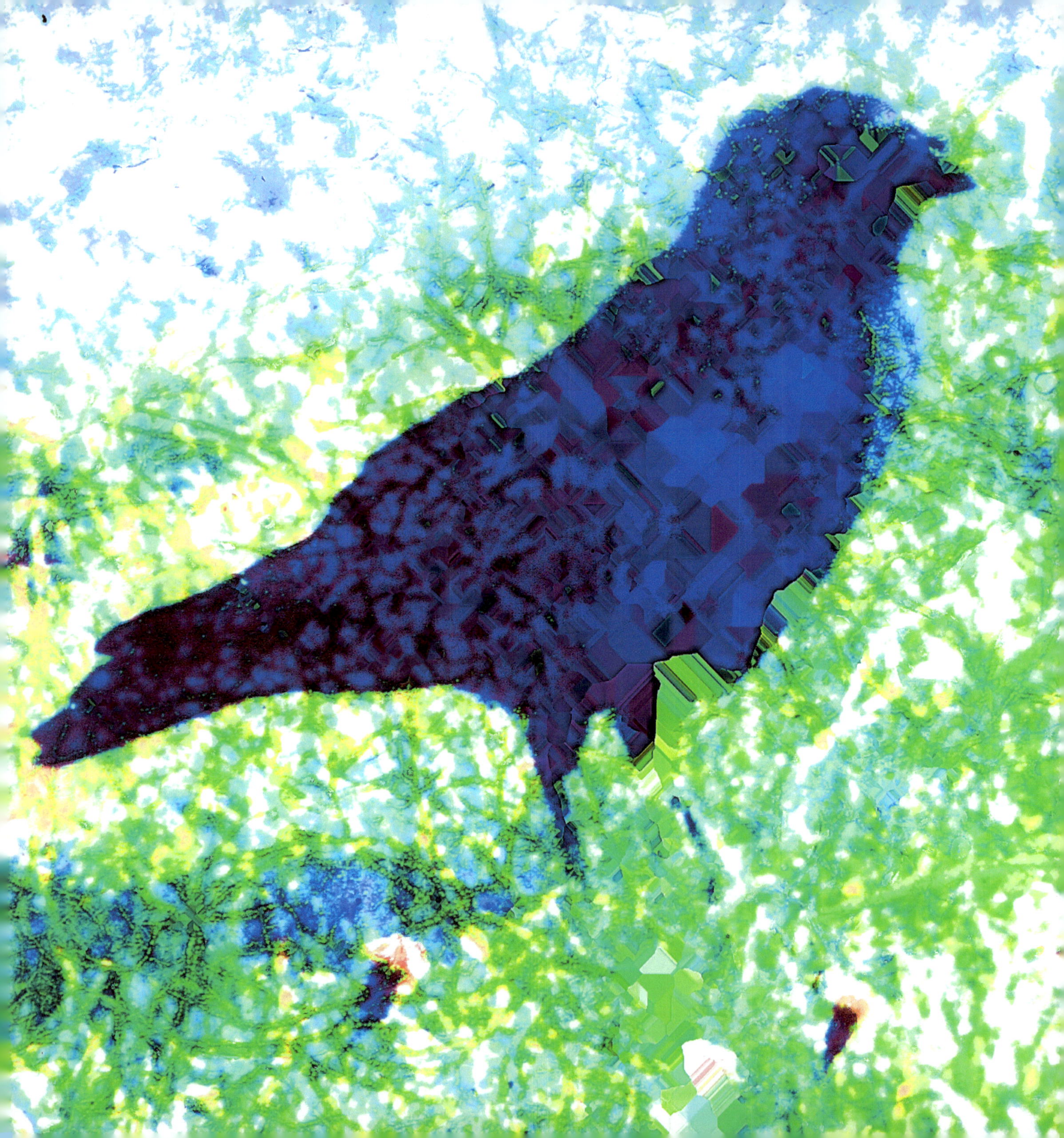

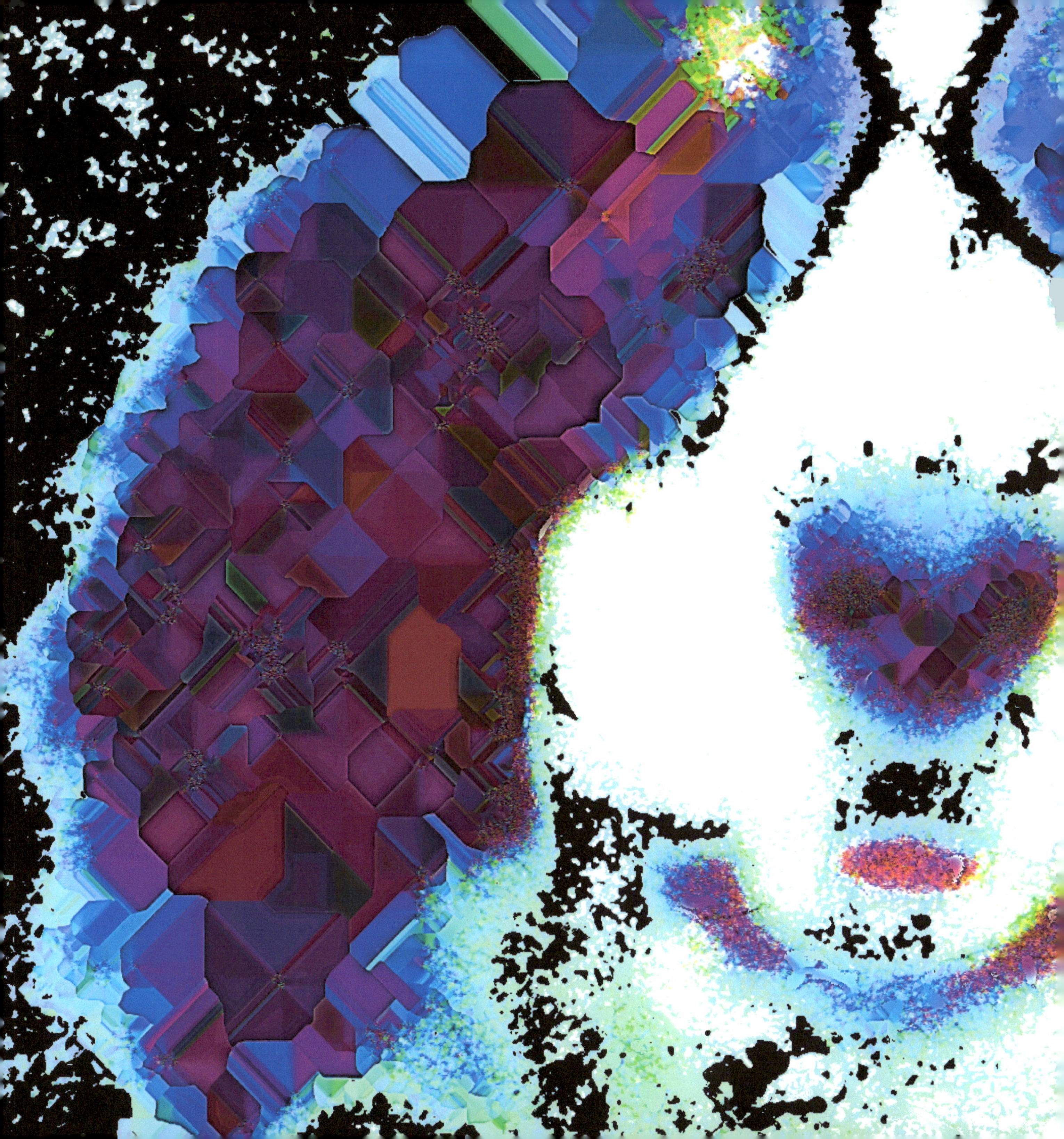

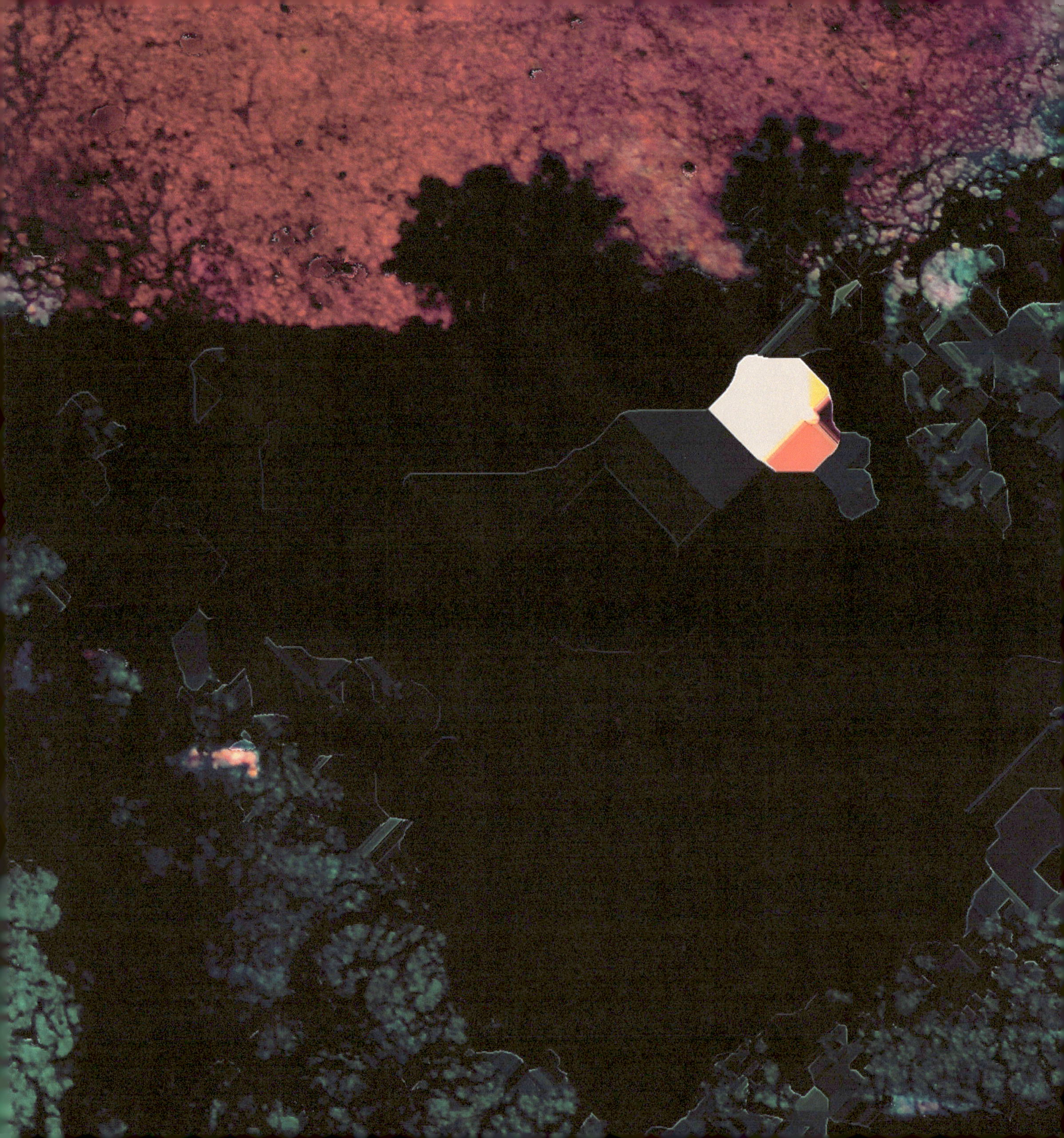

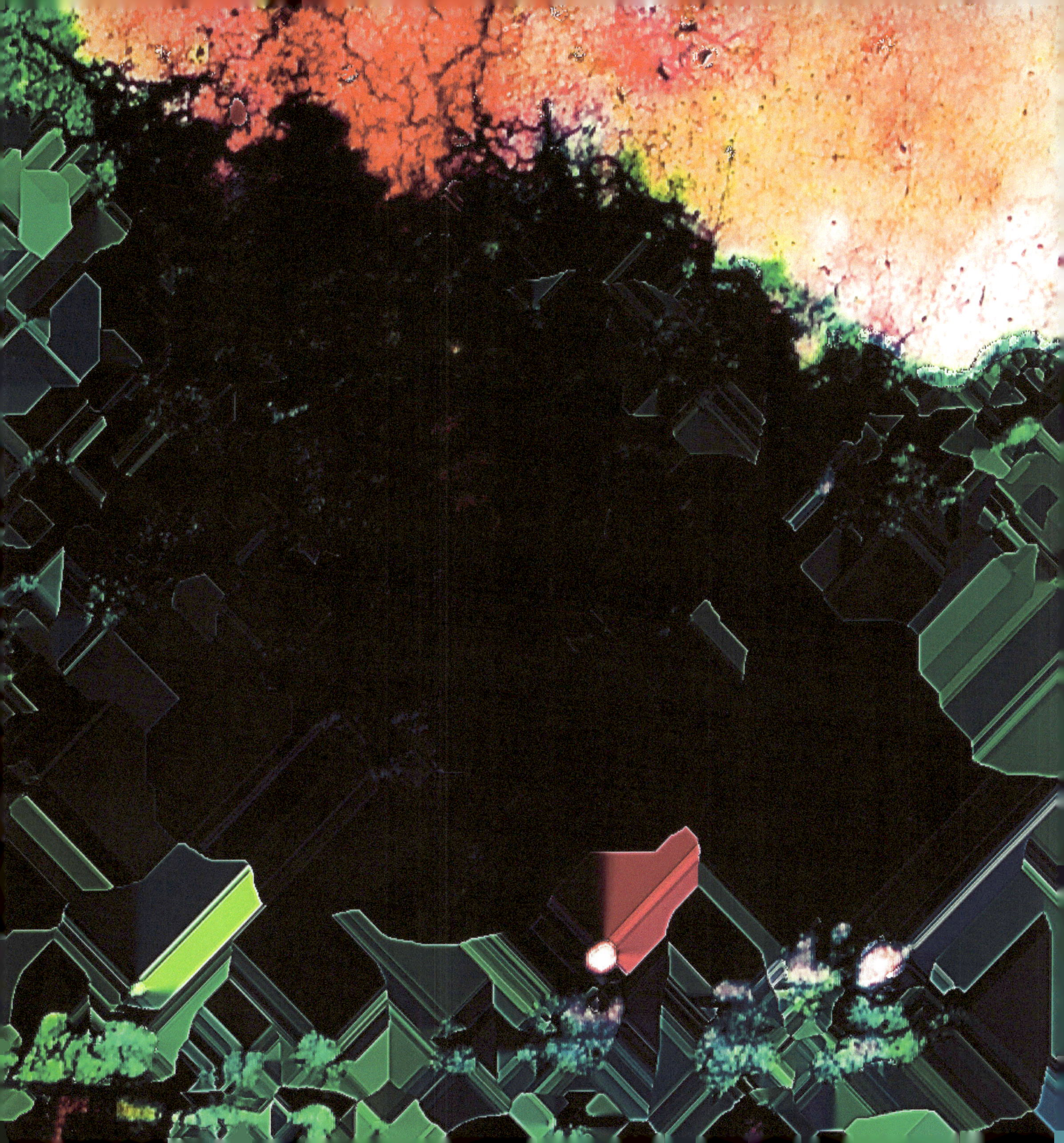

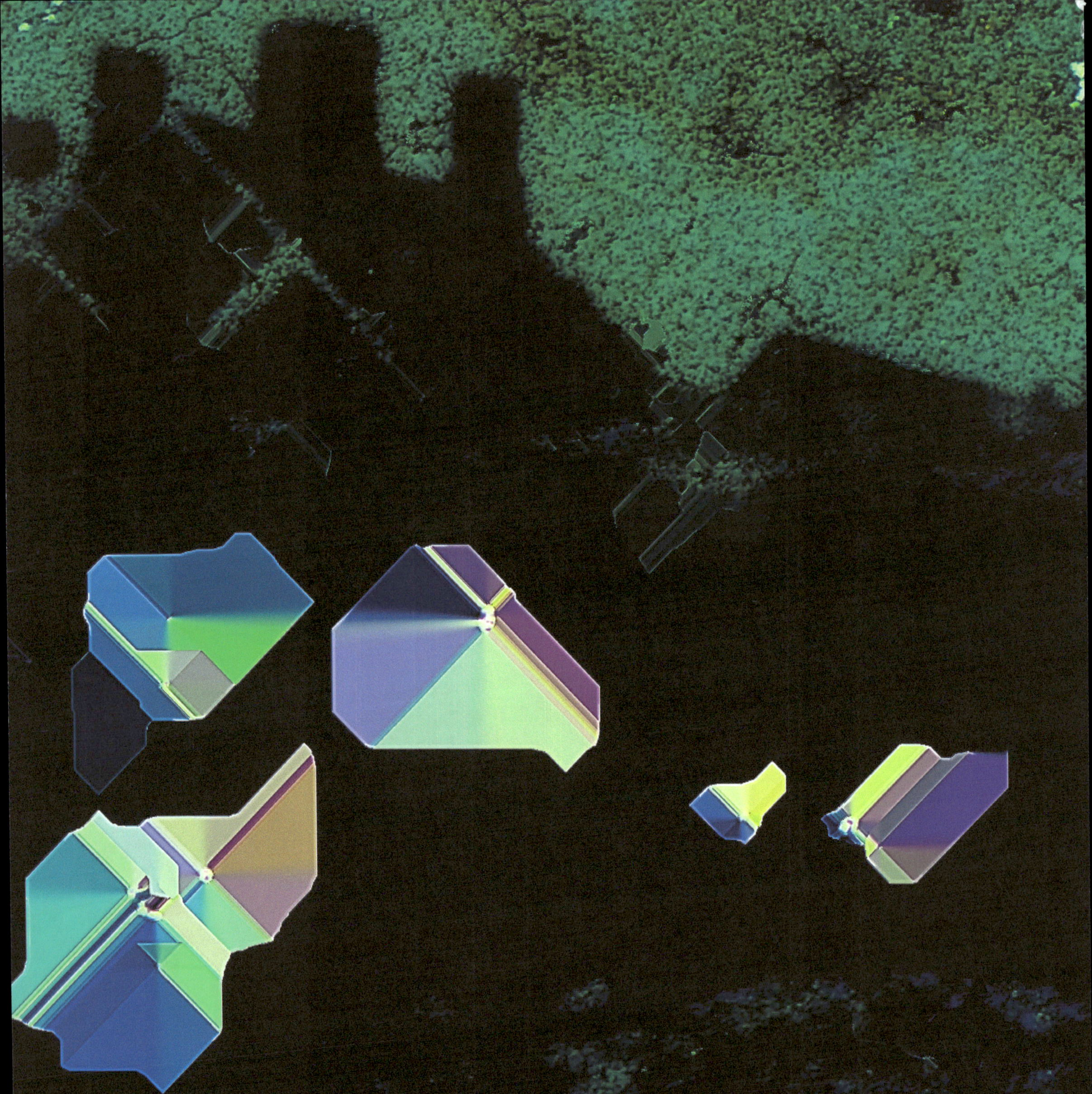

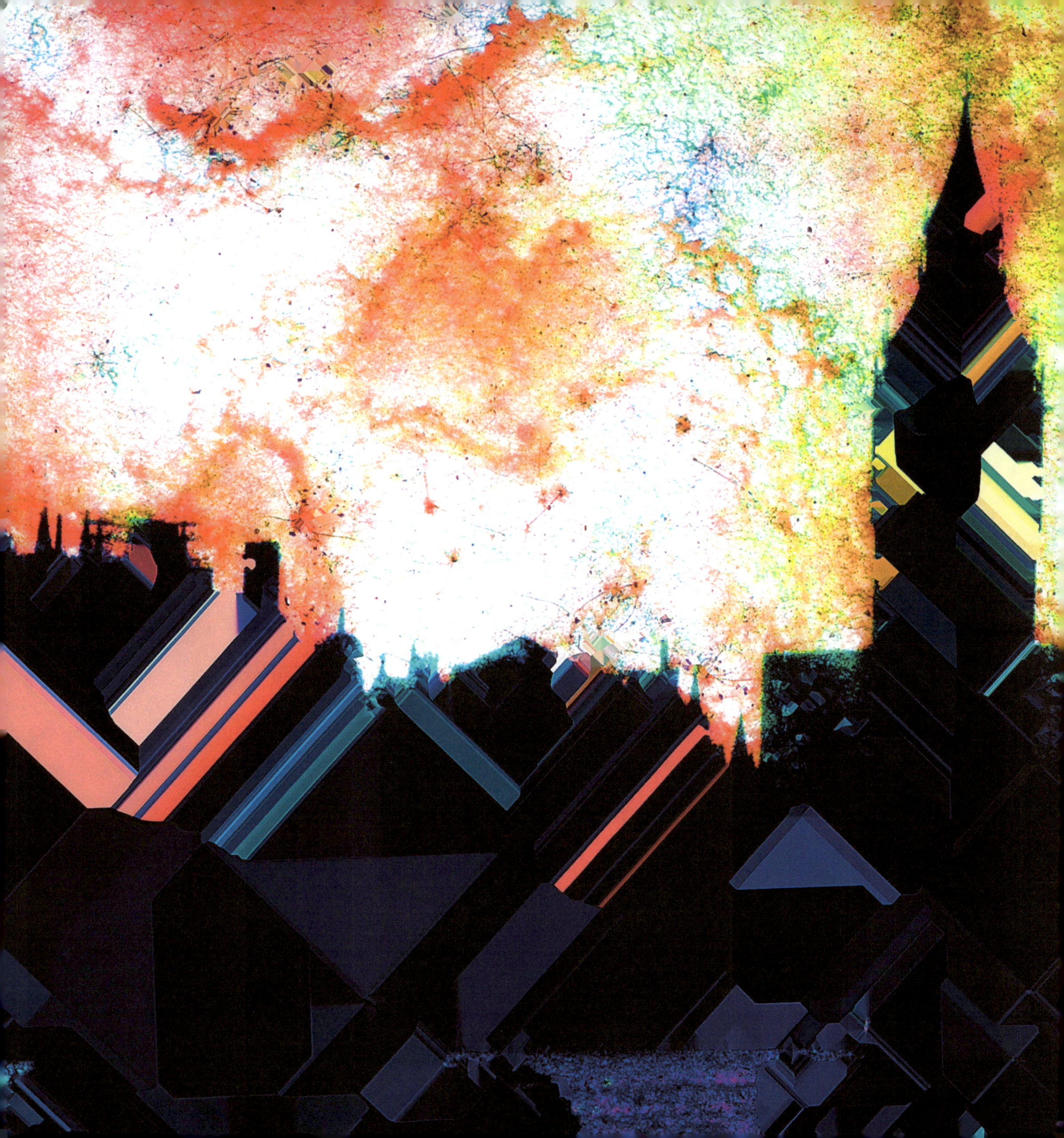

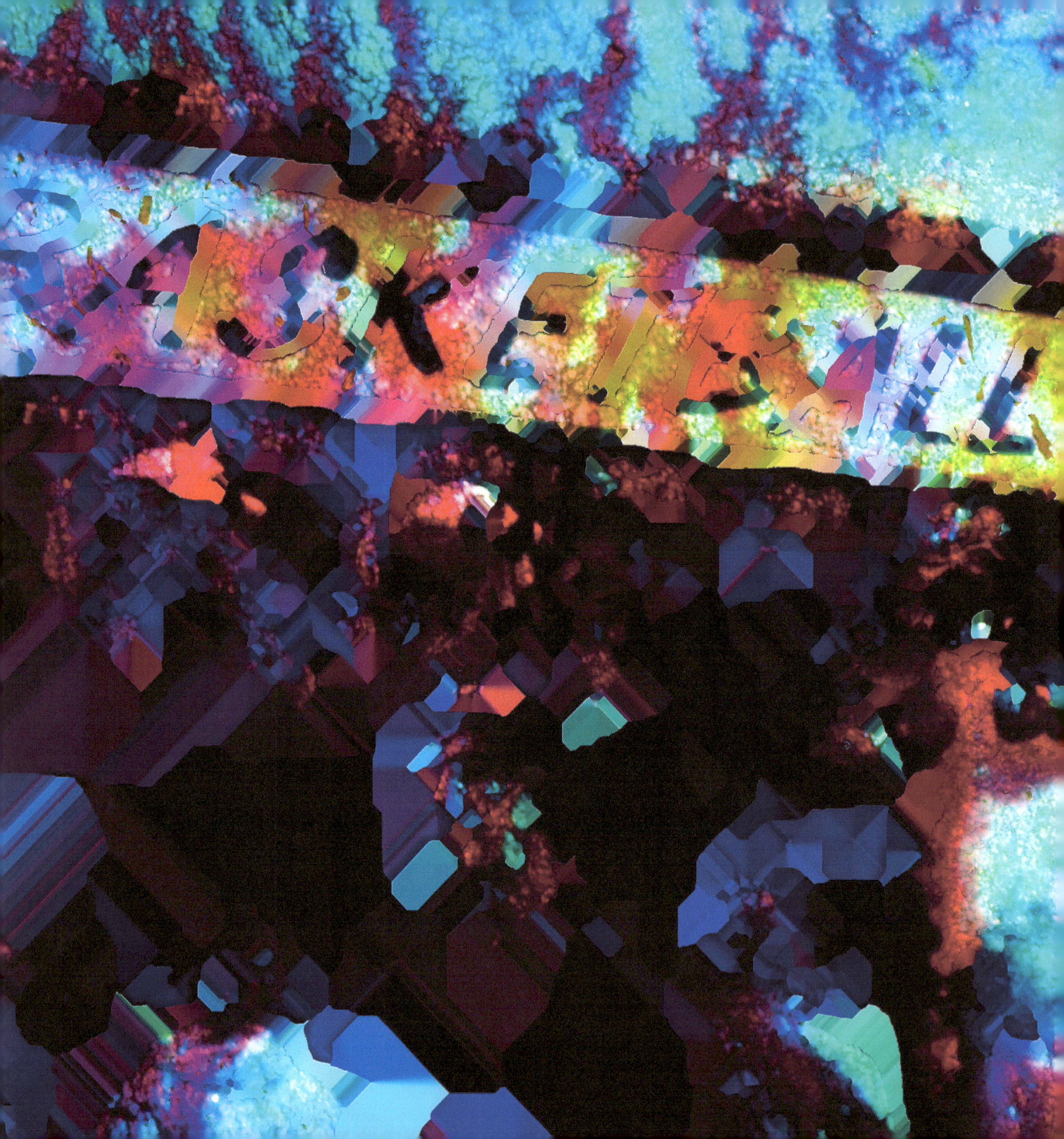

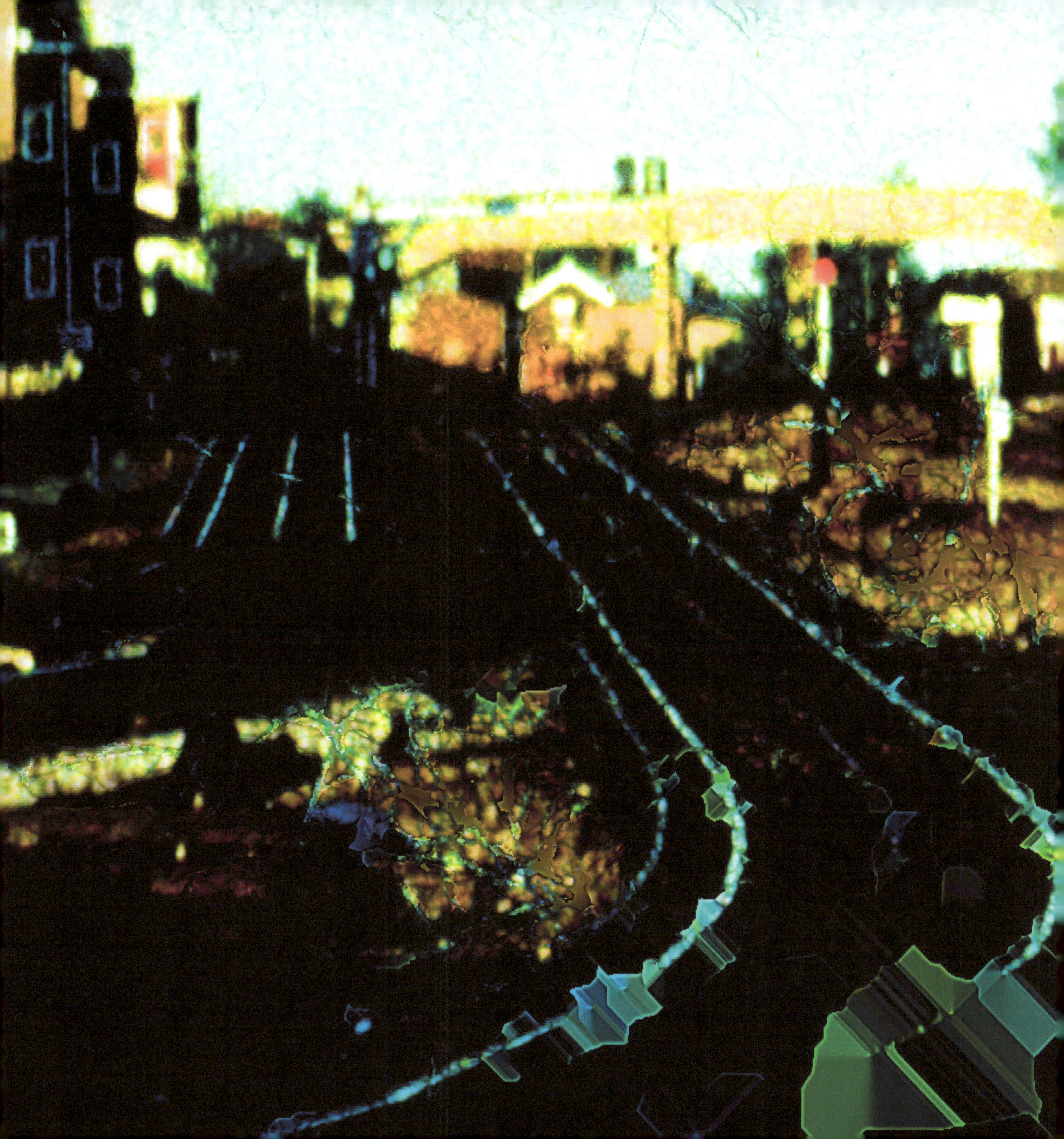

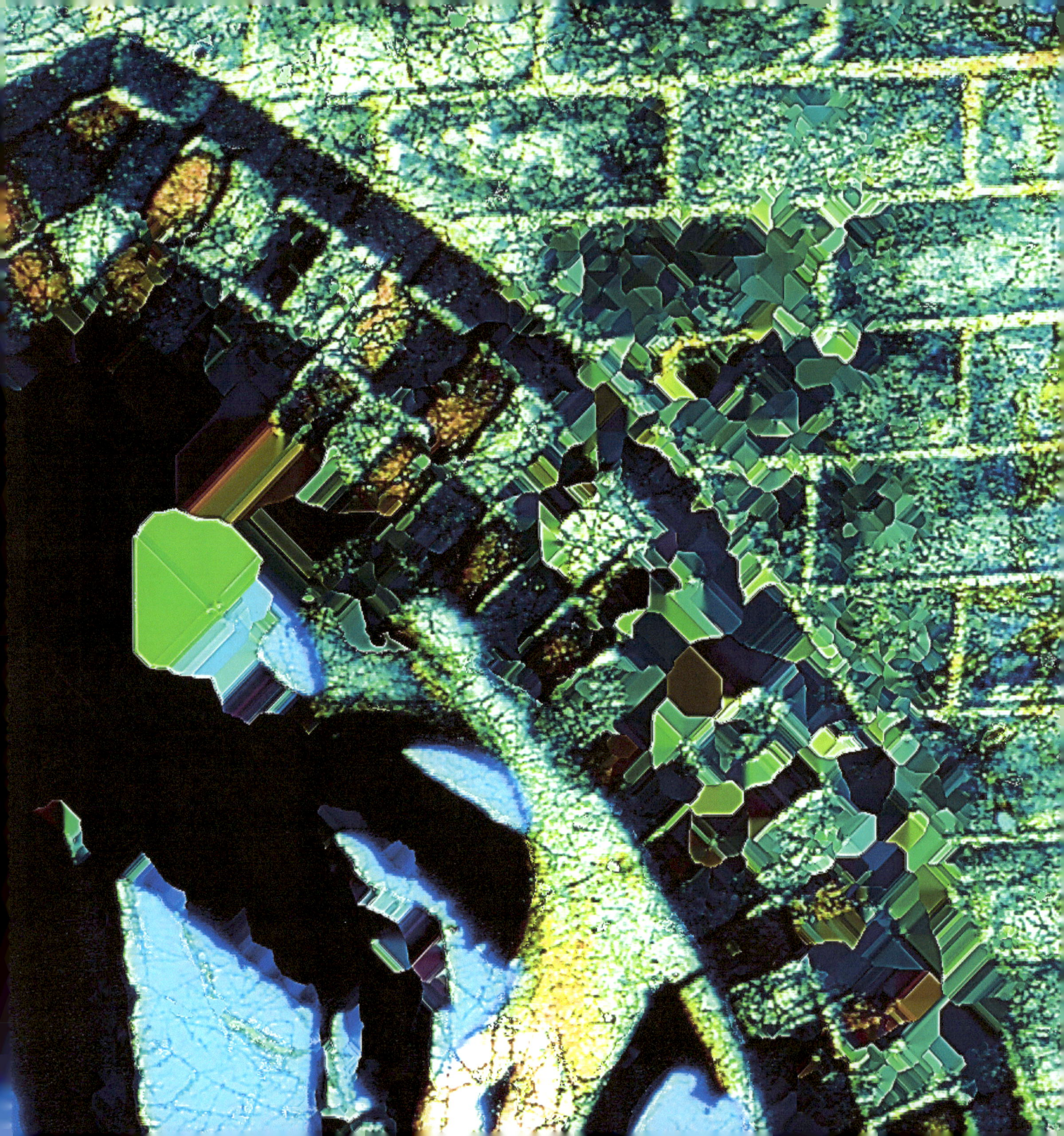

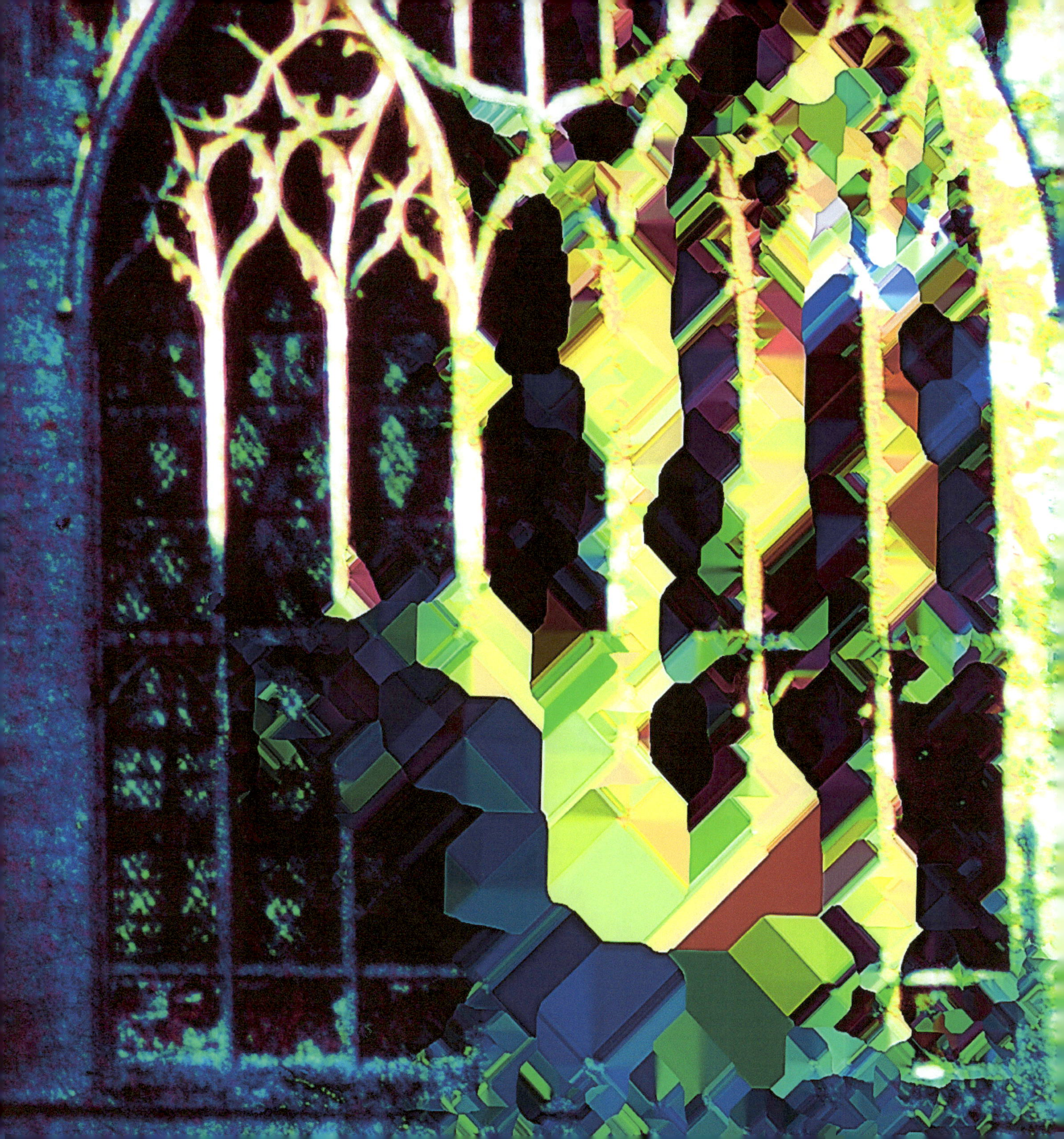

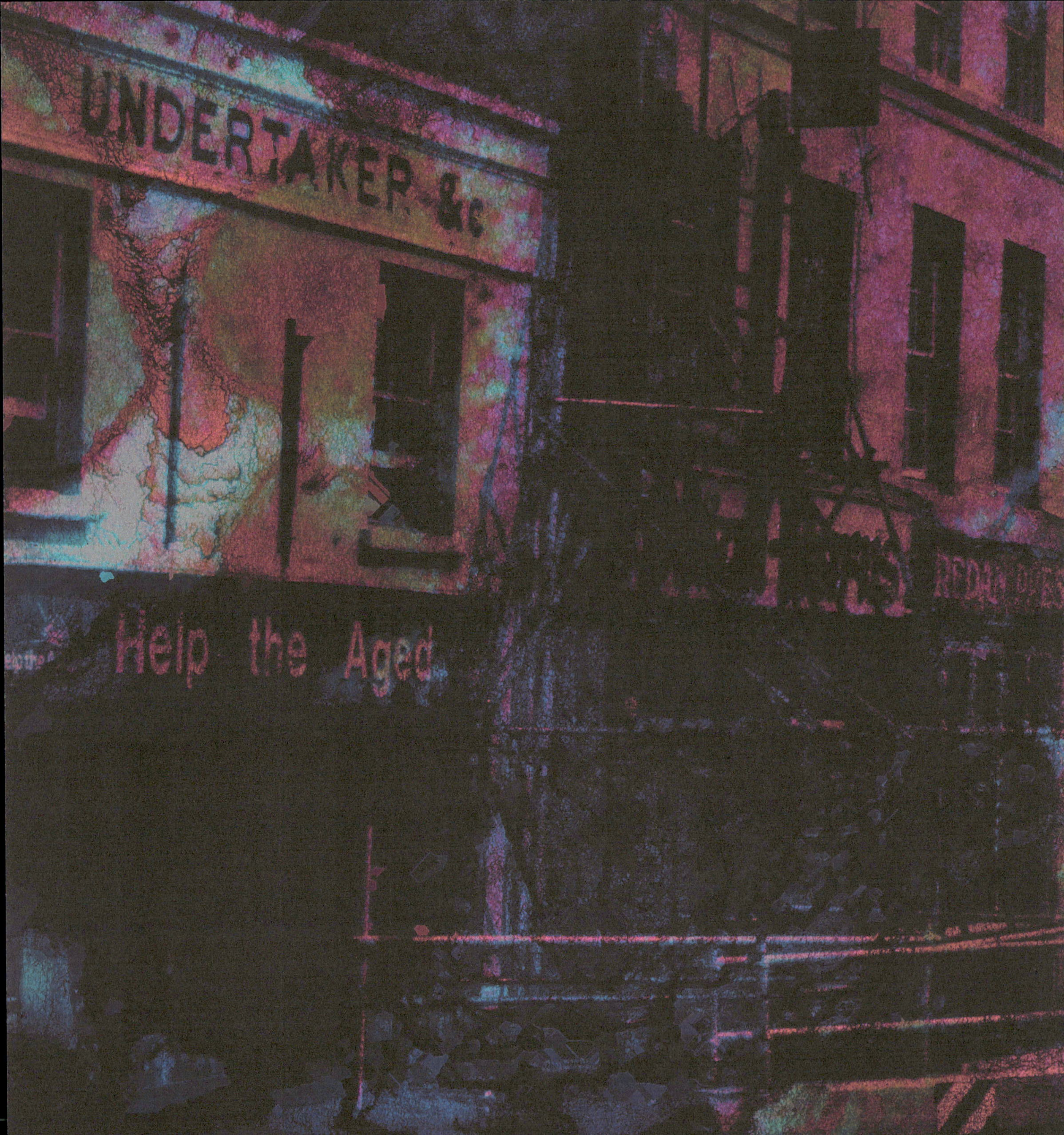

UNDERTAKER &c
Help the Aged

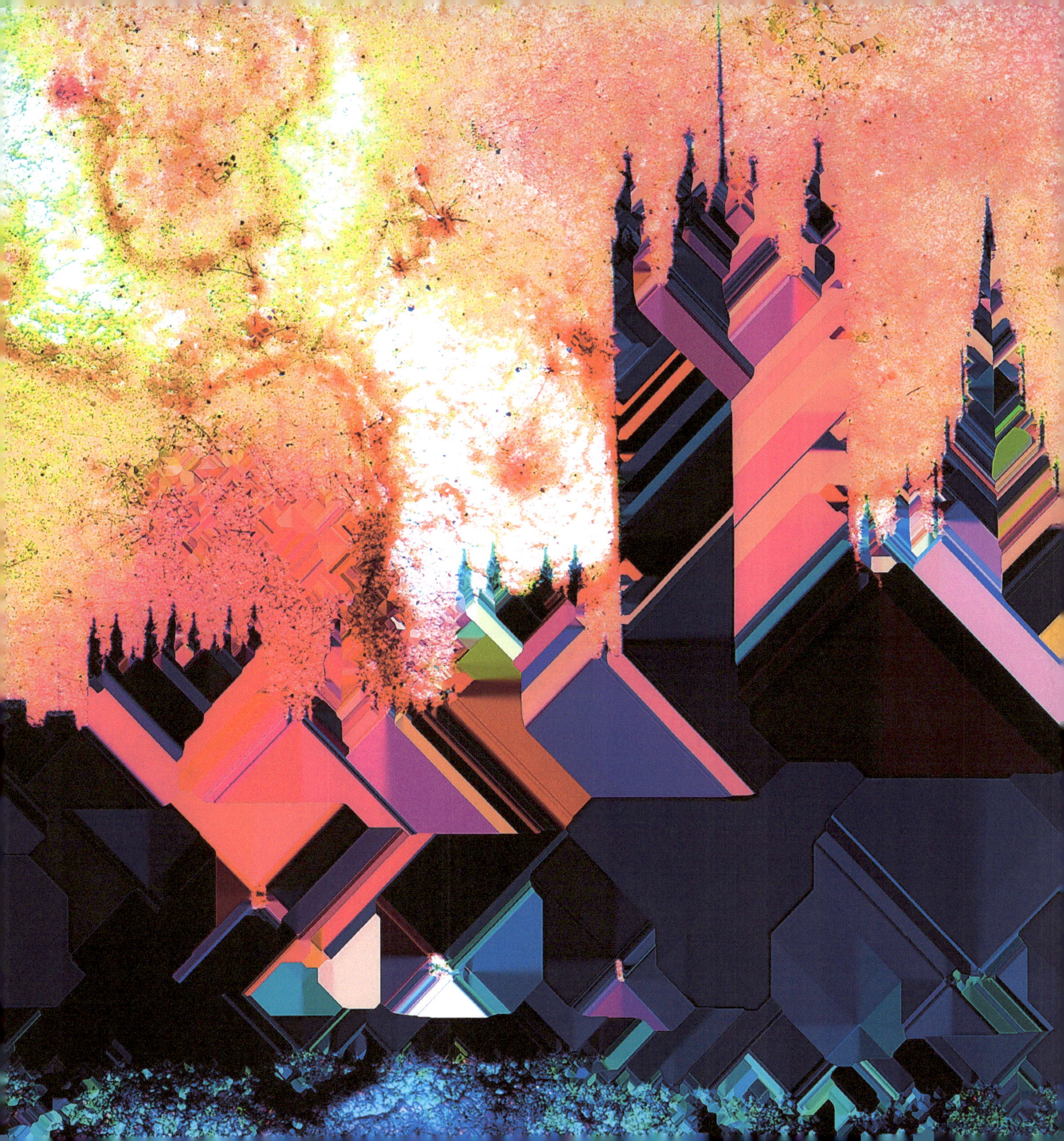

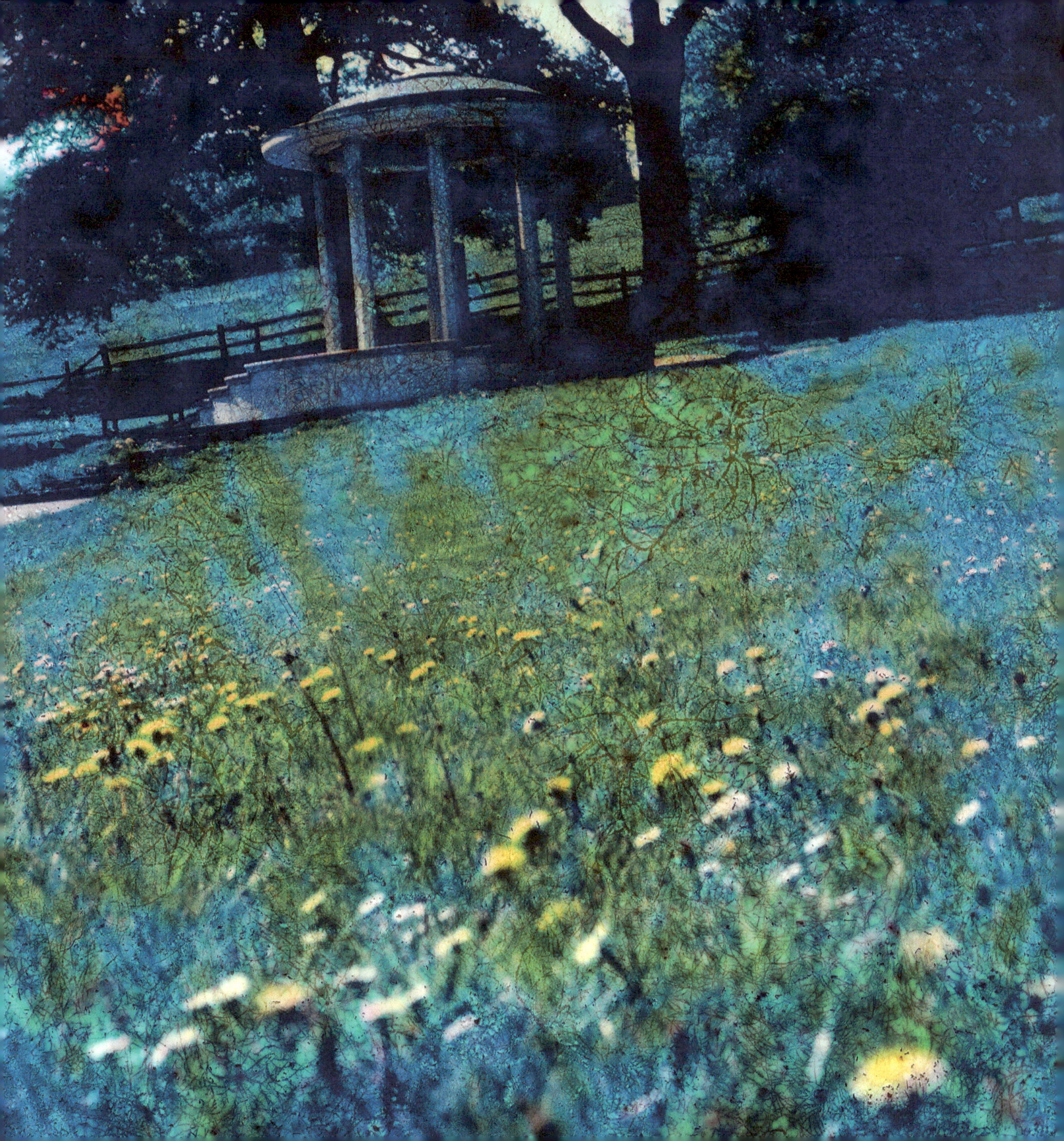

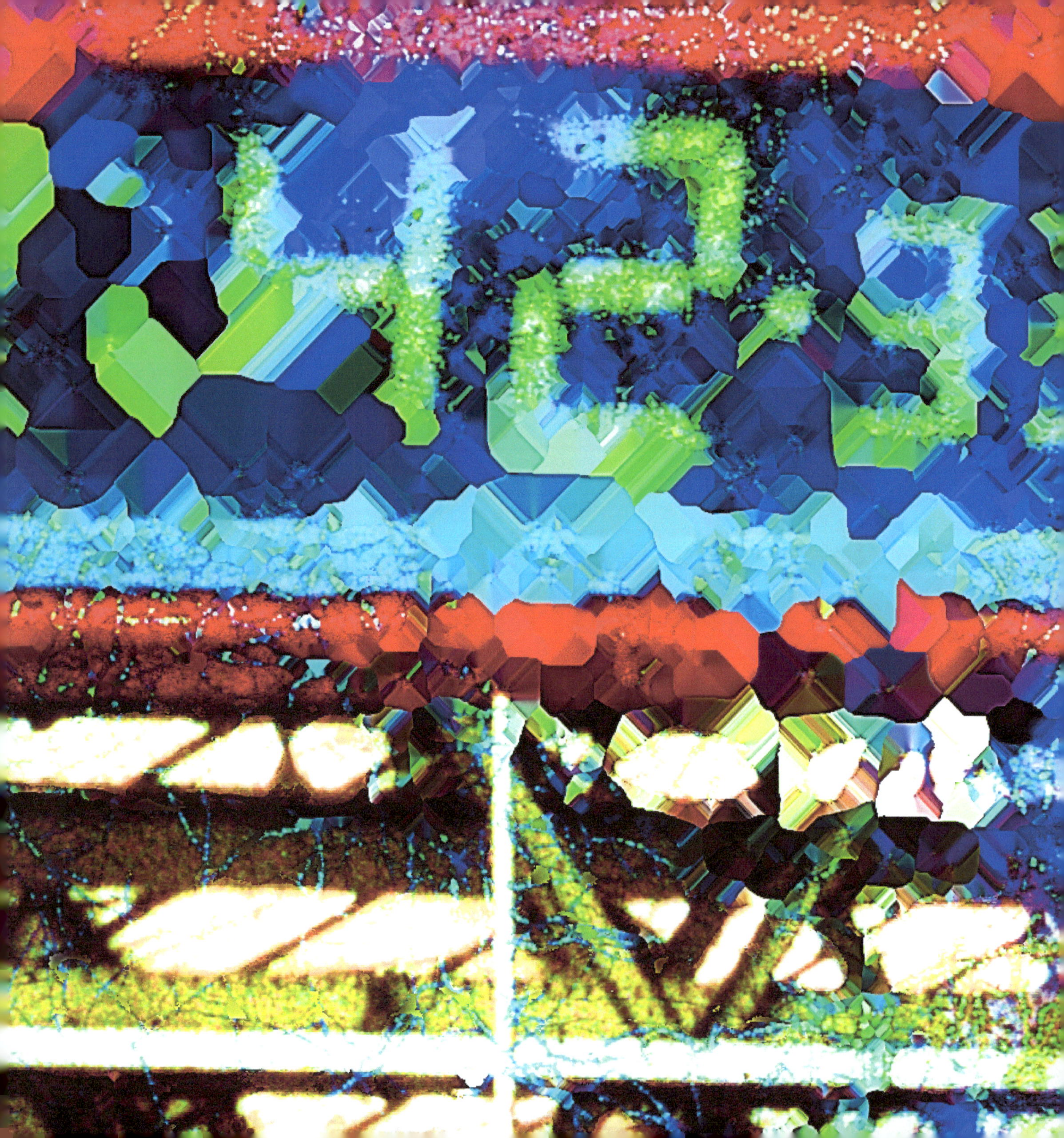

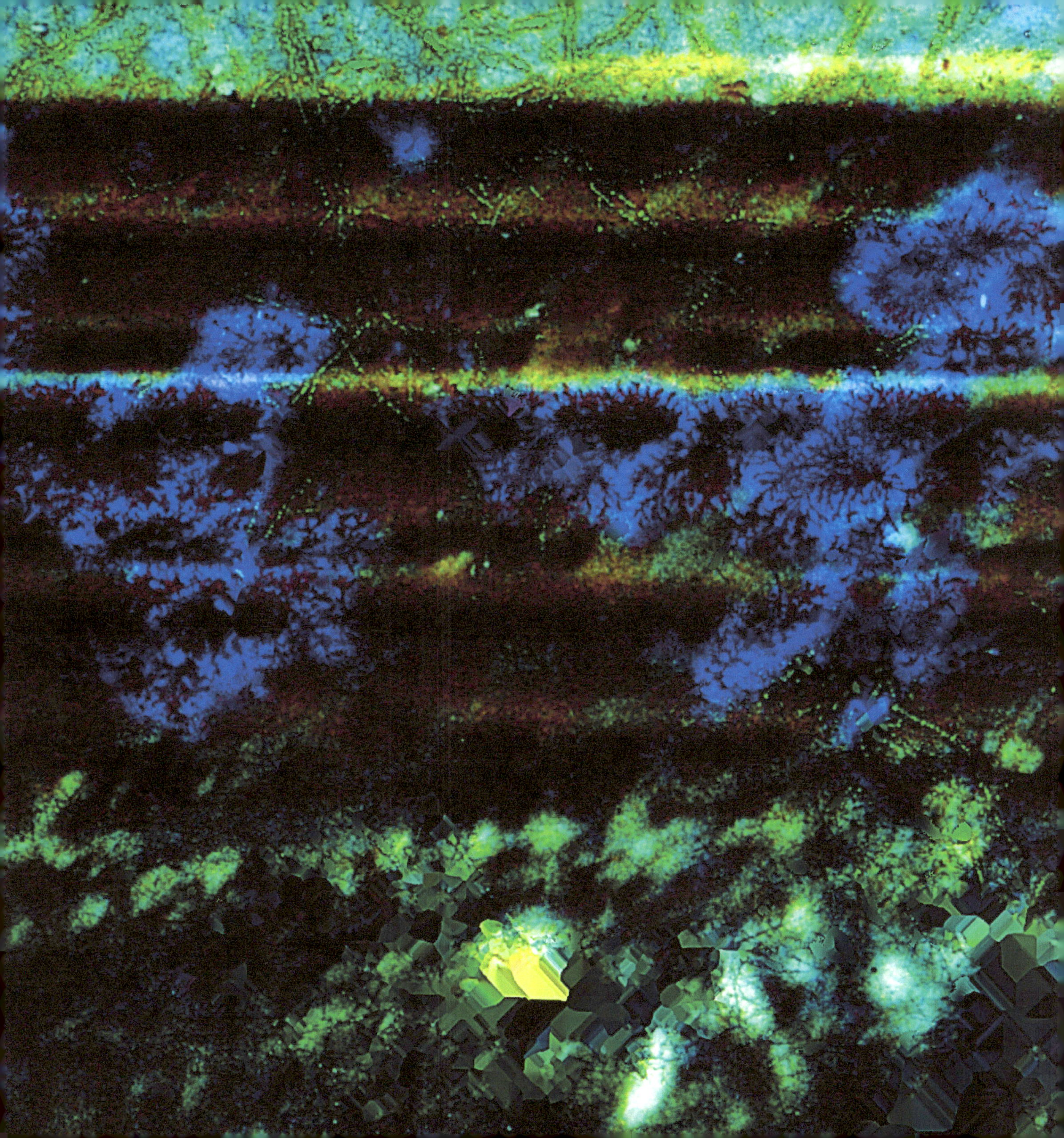

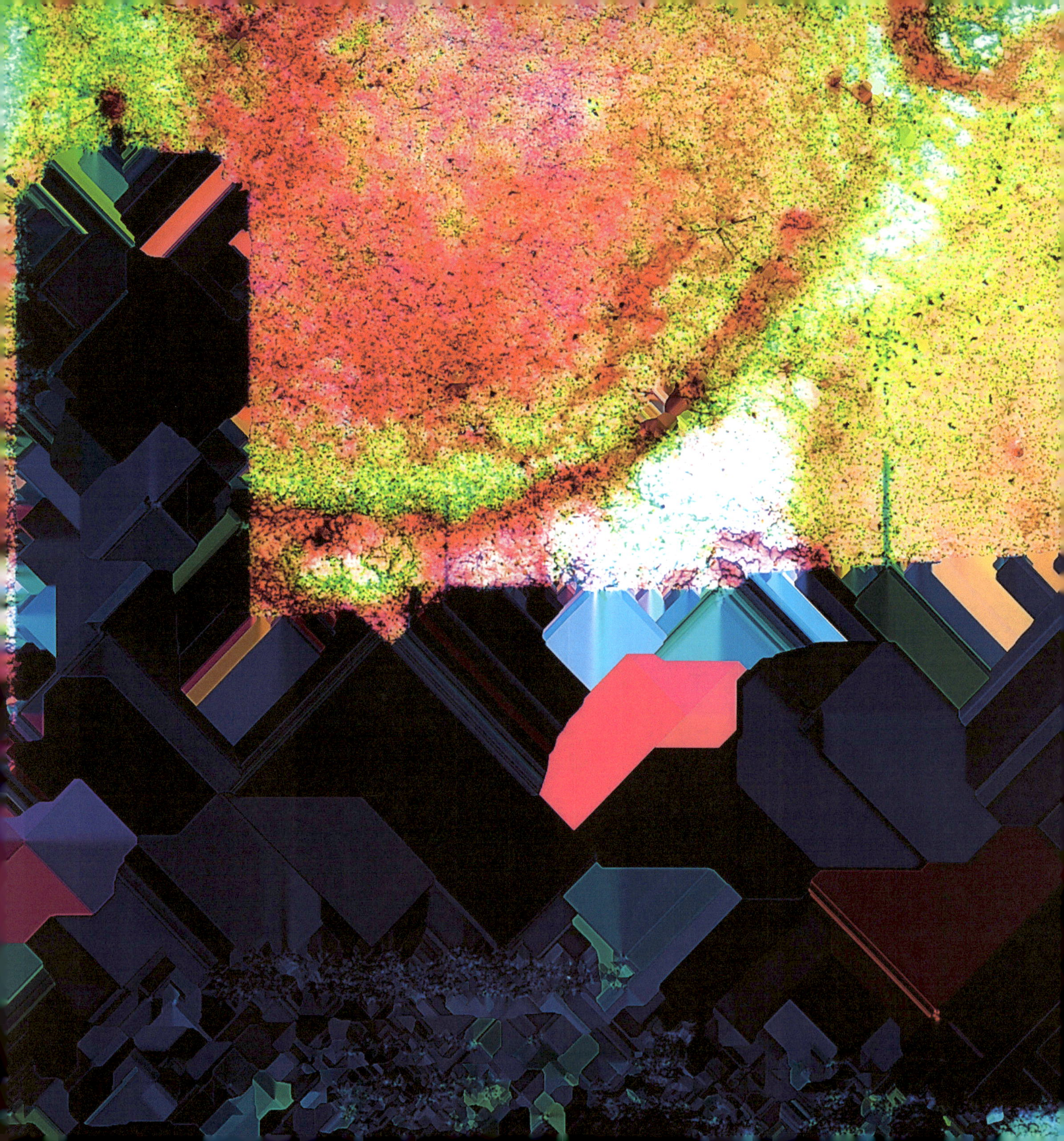

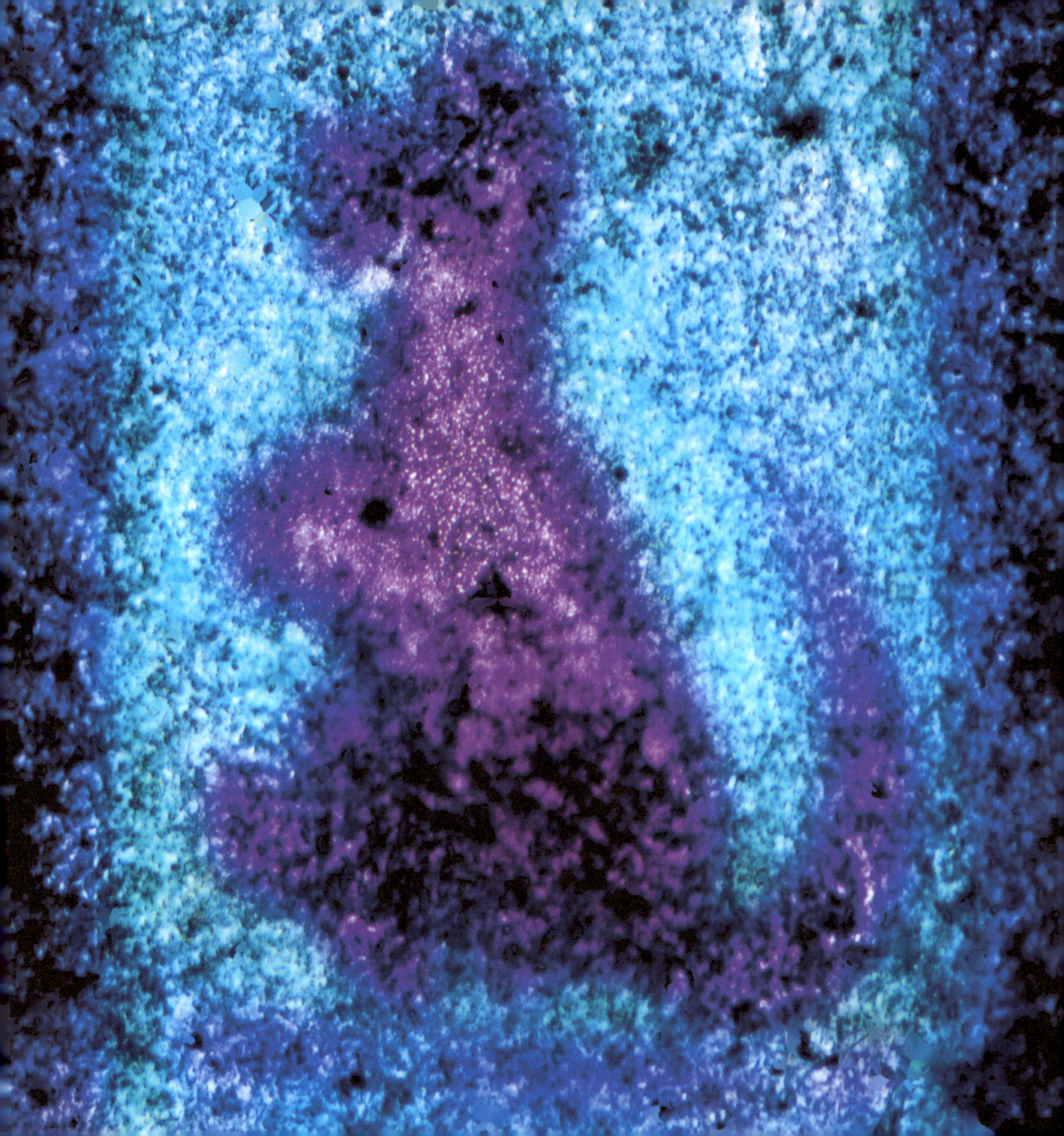

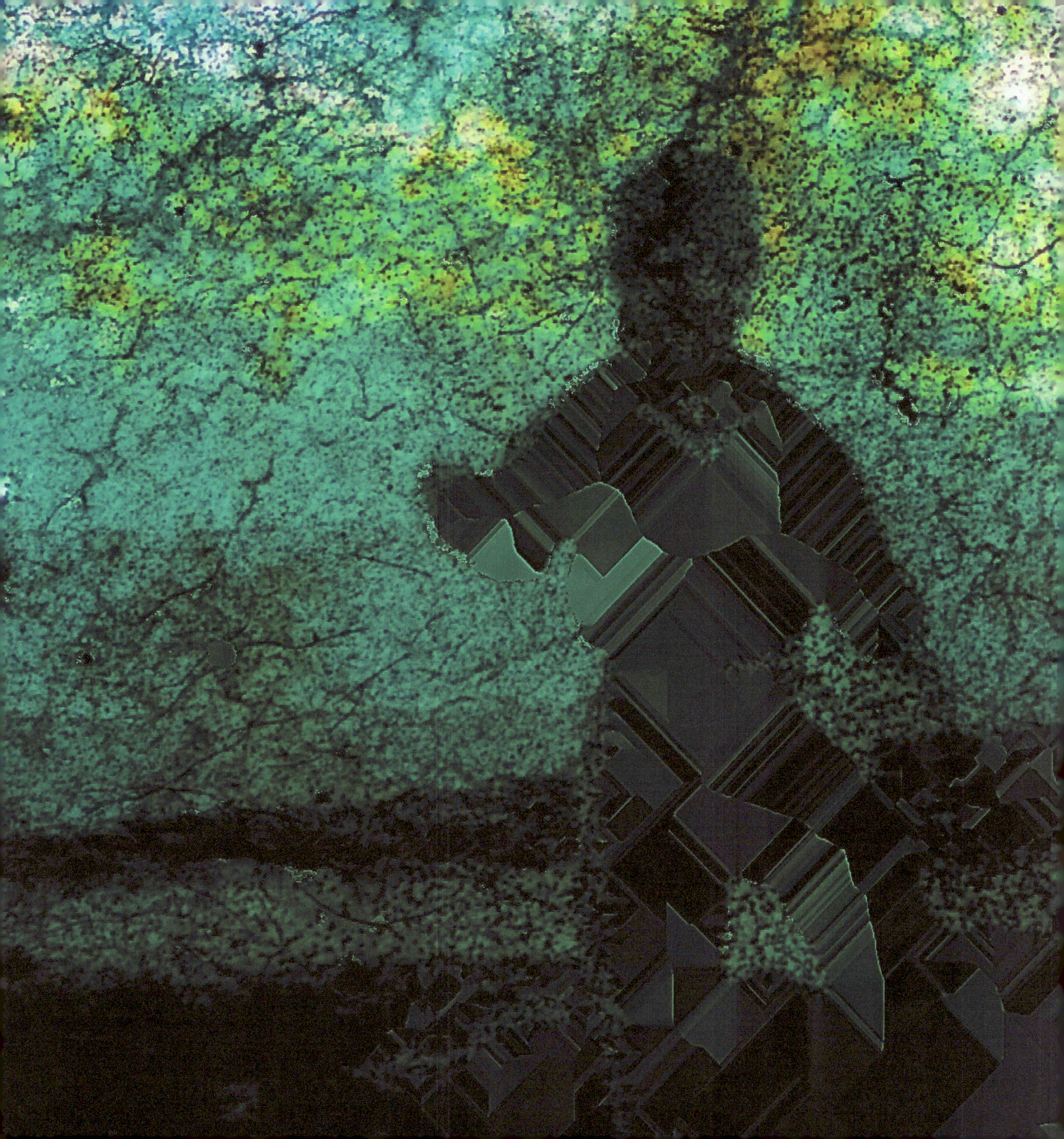

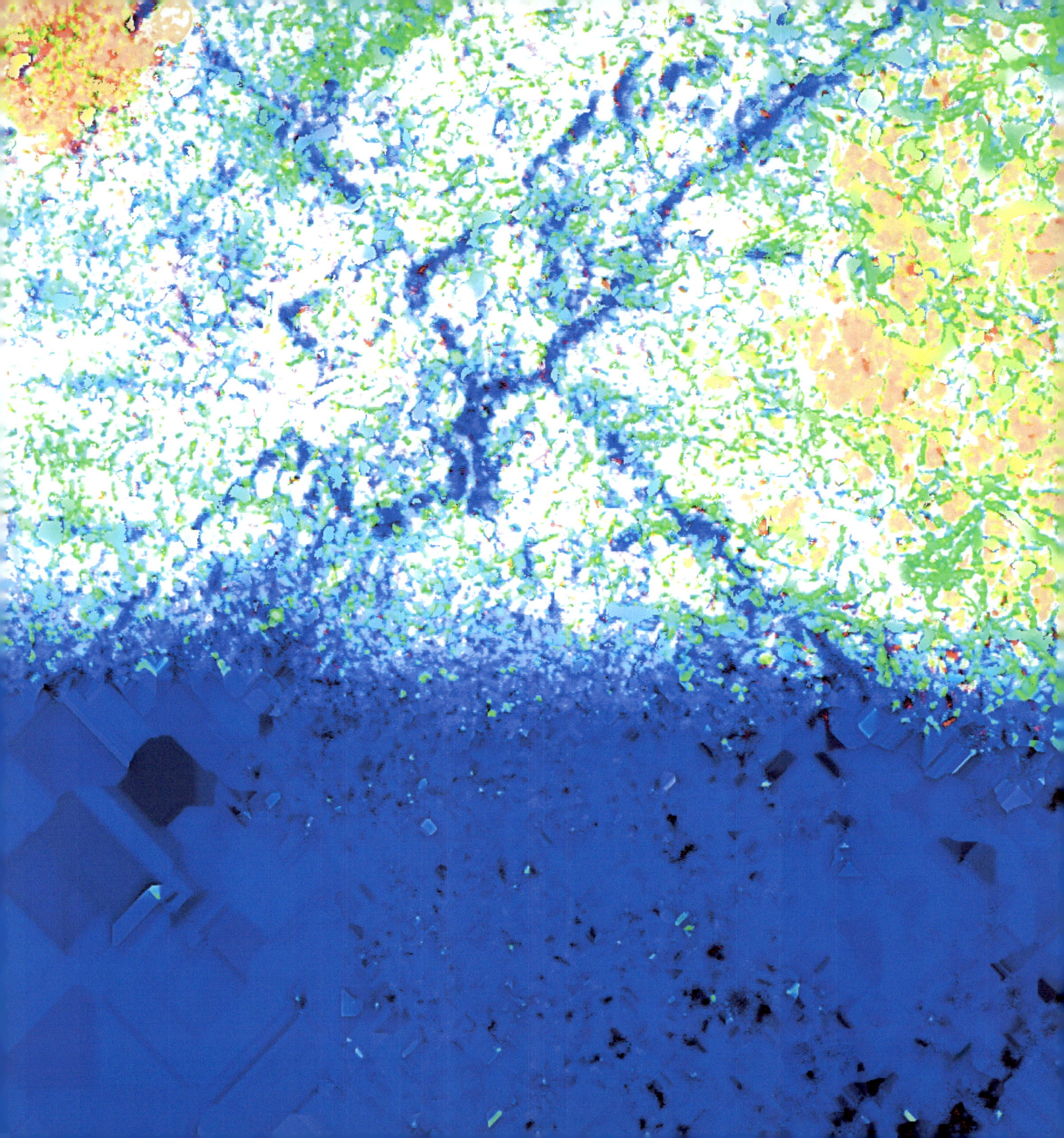

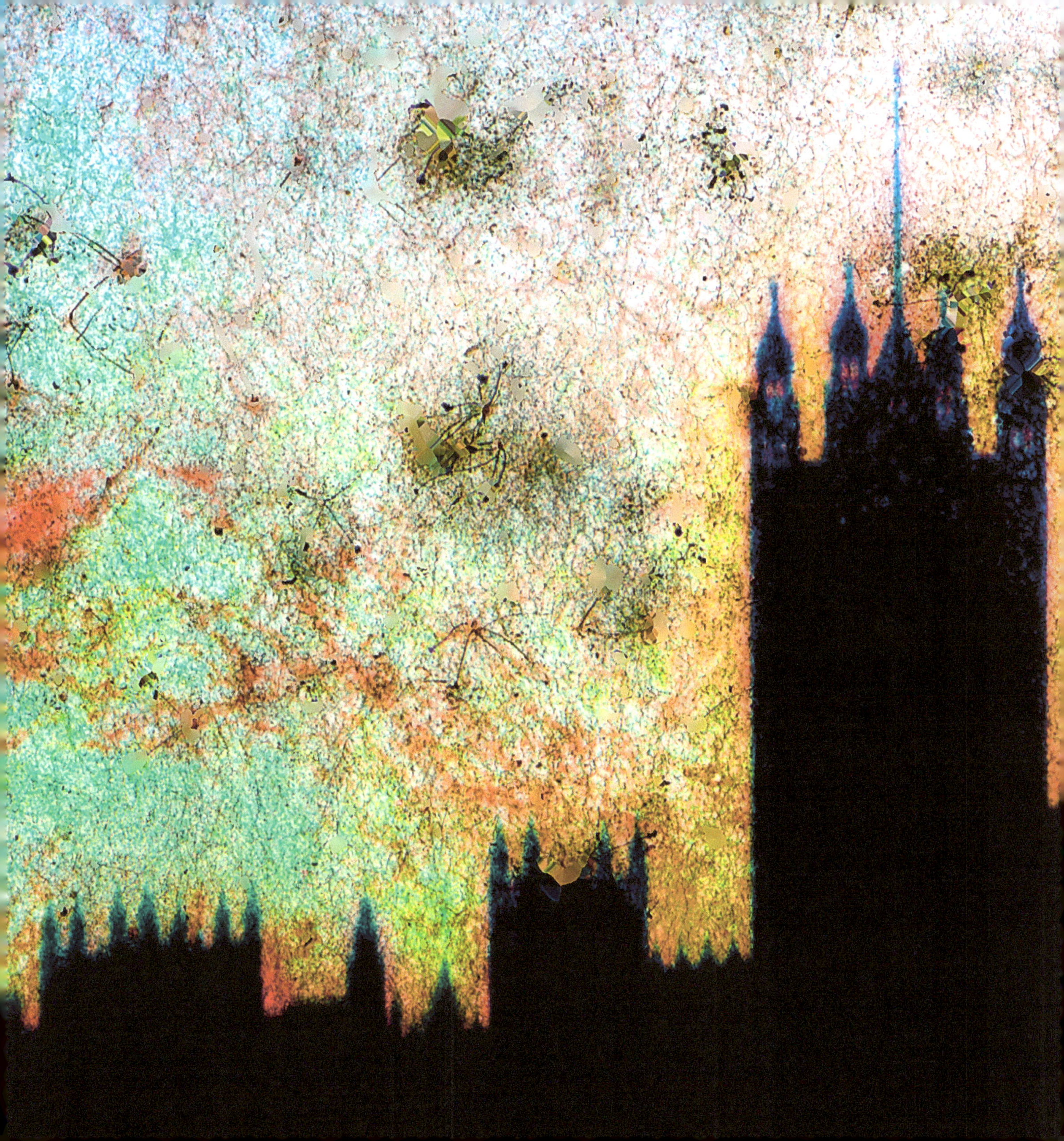

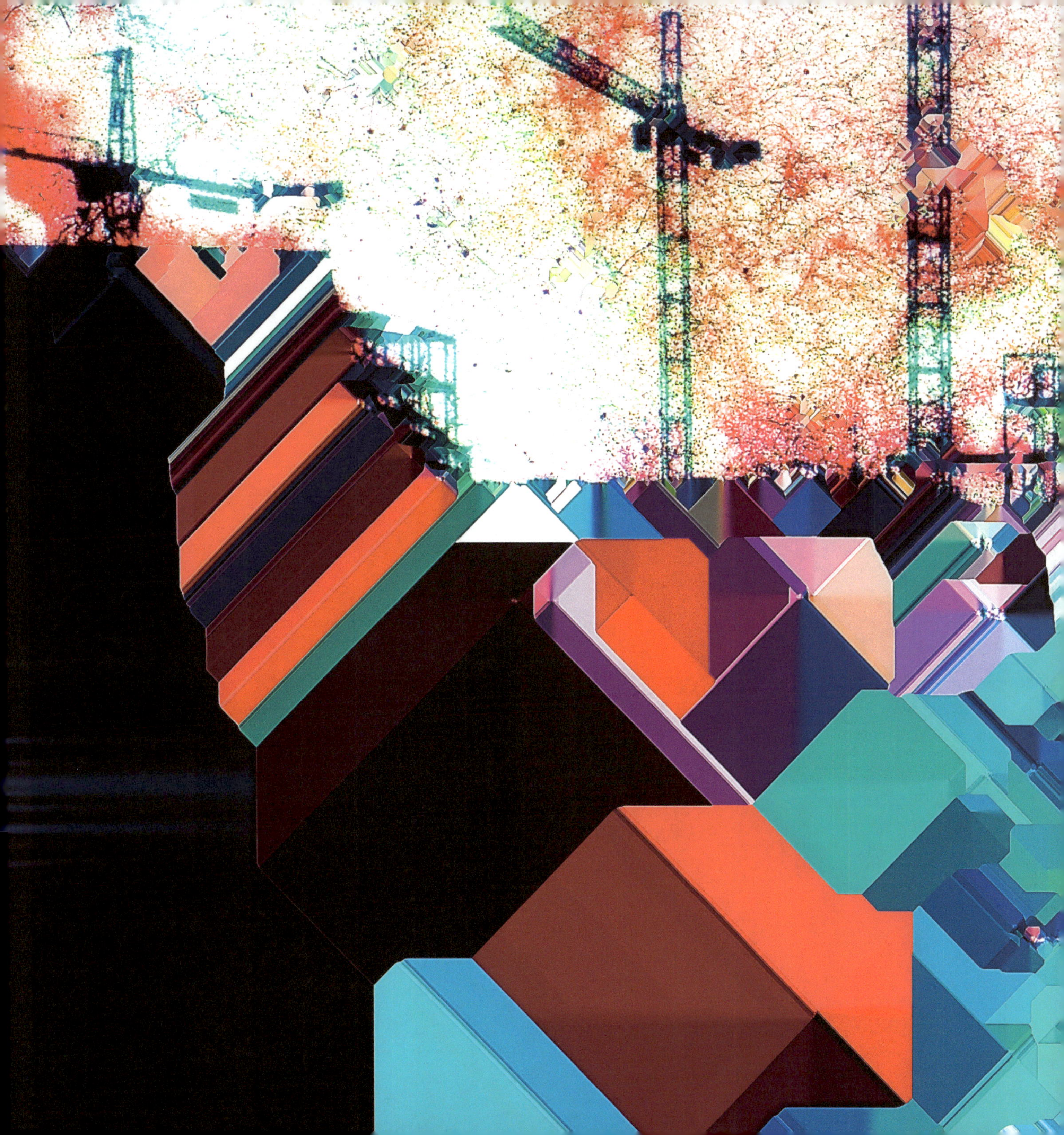

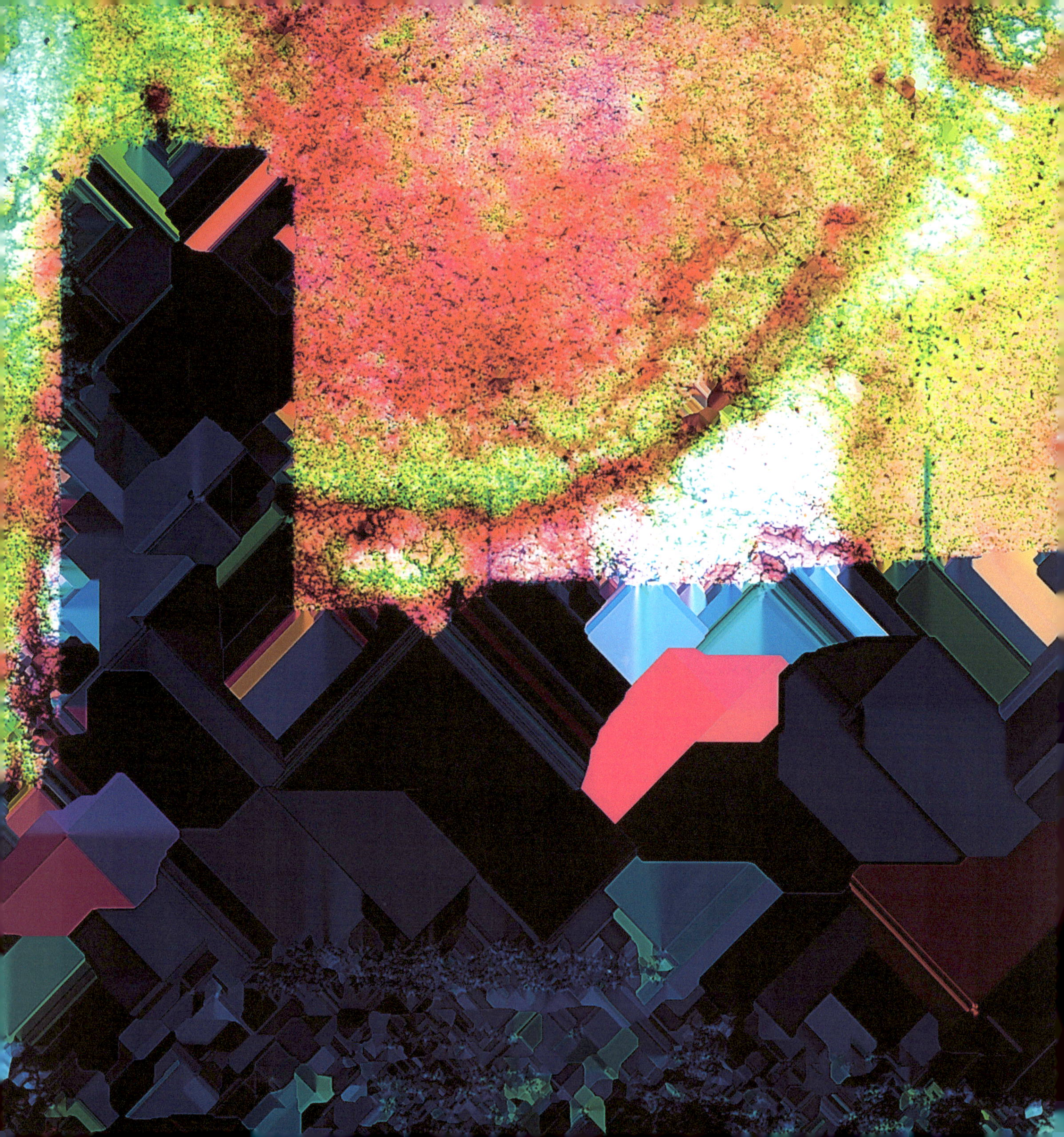

979-10-90394-91-9
dylan harris, corrupt press
82 rue du canal, 4051 esch-sur-alzette, luxembourg

première édition   septembre 2017
dépôt légal   septembre 2017
imprimé en france